Chasing the Butterfly

Chasing the Butterfly

The Pursuit of Meaning in Everyday Life

Barbara J Turner

Mountain River Publishing

Cover and book design: Beto Cumming

ISBN: 979-8-218-30828-5

Printed in the United States of America

Mountain River Publishing
Kingston, TN

In memory of Lawrence (Larry) Long
for inspiring confidence and courage in my writing

Introduction

> Don't be satisfied with stories,
> how things have gone for others.
> Unfold your own myth.
>
> —Rumi

As you read the book title, you are likely wondering how chasing a butterfly relates to the pursuit of life's meaning. You are the reader who will enjoy the metaphors and analogies in this collection of essays, poems, and verses that are the content of *Chasing the Butterfly: The Pursuit of Meaning in Everyday Life.*

Many people can identify with comparisons to transformation or growth or the phases of our lives that we describe as going through a metamorphosis. However, the butterfly's attributes representing freedom and wisdom are equally essential to our human journey. This book is about my endeavors to fulfill those longings.

As children, many of us literally chased a butterfly, hoping to capture the elusive creature. Intrigued by its beauty, the butterfly leads us in a game, darting from flower to flower. As adults, our proverbial chase becomes that of dream chasing. Like the butterfly of childhood, dreams often become just as elusive. But humans are resilient in adapting to change, so we press on.

Our aspirations entice us to continue exploring, which sometimes takes us out of our comfortable environment. By following hope's call of something better, we travel a path we might never have considered otherwise. Yet, with each venture, we learn more about who we are and what we want. Thus, we are led far beyond what we initially imagined. It is through the search that we find value and insight. The journey entices us with freedom, so we keep moving toward our goals as we try one more time.

Then, one day, something causes us to pause long enough to realize we may have overlooked the simple things that sustain our spirit while pursuing possibilities just beyond reach when what we long for is right where we are. While the butterfly's flight appears to be the ultimate in freedom, it can only drink the nectar required to sustain life when it becomes still.

As humans, we also savor our freedom; however, when we pause, we can reflect on our experiences and may discover that what we have been seeking finds us instead. The journey had to be taken to understand our purpose, but the path we travel teaches us many important lessons. Freedom allows us to go beyond our comfort zone, and new knowledge creates profound understanding, opening us to the magical. When we allow space for the unknown to surface, we find what logic cannot provide, leaving room for the mystery and the mystical to tie the pieces together.

Wisdom is always found in observing nature. Many of the essays in this book demonstrate ways to discover meaning and understanding in our surroundings. Pausing to reflect leads us to the connection in what nature has to teach us. Like the butterfly must pause to consume nectar, the mind can only connect to the wisdom within our soul in stillness, which illuminates understanding.

Contemplation allows the mind to get out of the way so we hear the soul speak. This practice is reflected in the essays, poems, and verses from my frequent pauses to embrace what I learned from chasing the elusive. There is vulnerability in opening one's heart and mind, yet rewarding through the realization that comes from the freedom in the journey. While there are many ways to do this, these practices work for me and are essential to my observations in *Chasing the Butterfly: The Pursuit of Meaning in Everyday Life.*

In whatever way you choose to seek it, the meaning is in the journey. I hope you enjoy reading my reflections, and I wish you a mystical chase.

Art of Allowing

The Art of Allowing

It is too early to be up and contemplating the mysteries of life and the universe. I am no longer sleepy, so it is time to begin my day.

The rain and fog of the past few days have blocked my view of the full moon, but I know it's there. I'm sitting in the dark because I don't want to waste a moment of the beauty of the moonlight-infused fog surrounding me. I am part of the great mystery.

These things are my teachers. While the full moon is shrinking and moving away from me, every cell in my body knows I am here to learn. The fog will lift, and the river will still be underneath it, moving with purpose toward the ocean.

Why is it so hard to allow these lessons to lead me? The water in the river does not fight the current; instead, it relaxes into the flow, fulfilling its intention without effort. The fog, likewise, does not engage in a battle to remain when conditions change. It does not linger to contemplate the physics of how fog disappears. It does not say let me think about this a minute until I understand why this is happening.

As the first-born child of two first-born parents, I will likely maintain the tradition of that personality type, so I may never master my over-achieving tendencies. I am confident that I will think about why I feel compelled to understand the meaning of everything again.

My thoughts return to the scene around me, and I put down my pen. The fog has advanced toward me and wrapped me in its cool caress. As the moon drops behind the western horizon, I allow myself to fully become part of this mysterious happening.

A New Song

I hear the rain beginning as I wake from dreams that punctuated my sleep with freshness, dreams of new people, places, and activity, although I do not remember the details. This feeling has varied but is recurring since I returned from a writers' retreat last week. My dreams are usually ones of problem-solving, but recently I have been a participant in, and the originator of, this infusion of newness. Leftover feelings from dreams are of change, excitement, and attainment.

A flash of lightning brightens the darkness as a boom of thunder shakes the house. The dreams fall from my sleep. As they shatter and break, I become fully awake to the sounds and light display from the powerful storm raging outside.

I sit in the darkness and feel the storm's energy as I think of these ideas that have invaded my sleep. What do they portend, if anything at all? Thoughts of the absence of problems that need solving and the sheer opportunities are refreshing like a storm leaves rain behind to soothe the thirsty landscape.

As thunder and lightning briefly subside, the tiny wren that lives under the deck begins to sing her morning melody. Perhaps she, too, feels the newness and is reminding me that my turn to sing has also arrived.

I settle into the comfort of that thought as the storm intensifies again, and the wren retreats in silence to wait it out. I am mindful that my turn will come just as calm follows a storm and day follows night. The rain stops again, and the wren reappears, singing her song as if it belongs solely to her.

Free From Yesterday

The raindrops that lulled me to sleep last night are not the same as the ones that greeted my awakening today, yet both offer cleansing for the soul. The night's raindrops soothe and diminish the cares of the day, transporting me to peaceful sleep. As I awaken, their soft melody smooths entry into a new day, free from yesterday with its concerns over things left undone, offering one more chance to get it right.

Colors of Evening

Last evening, I watched as the day began its transition to night. I had intended to watch from the deck as I enjoyed early dinner. Although the thermometer registered 58 degrees, the breeze made the air feel colder. The wind chimes seemed to take no notice of the chill in the air and played a soft, sparkling melody in appreciation. But the cold became too much, so I retreated to watch from inside.

From the warmth of the sunroom, I continued to enjoy the soft colors of the evening as the clouds reflected changes from the angle of the setting sun as it dropped below the ridges in the West. I was elated when I saw the flash of the brilliant white head of a bald eagle as he fished for dinner along the shoreline. Does he see the beauty of the sky that surrounds him? Or is he focused solely on catching his meal?

Soon the trees will have donned their summer leaf cover and will hide much of the river from my view at this level. But for now, I will enjoy the evening colors along the river as I watch the ever-changing scene before me.

It is magical to be alive at this time of day when the sky is awash in hues from the Master's palette, and a soft breeze stirs the trees. Another eagle appears, but this one is immature, floating gracefully along as he makes his way upriver.

As night falls, I allow my mind to wander freely, where memories flood my heart just as tomorrow's sunrise will do to the shadows of the night.

A Frog Is My Teacher

All is quiet in the pre-dawn. The symphony of katydids that sang me to sleep last night is silent, and the frog soloist on the deck has concluded his throaty song, turning his attention now to the bugs that have accumulated in the corners.

This early morning silence is deafening as night fades from the sky. In the quiet, I can hear my heart open to accept the voices of uncertainty and wisdom, which seem in conflict. They are simultaneously separate and the same in the ebb and flow of life's river, moving me toward some destination not yet revealed to me. Staying present takes constant awareness, even as my mind always wants to move faster.

While he concentrates on the bugs, the frog is not concerned that he was not in tune with last night's katydid concerto, nor is he thinking ahead about this evening's performance. Instead, he is enjoying breakfast that he had to do nothing to get except show up. He inherently knew food was available when he was ready to eat. He had no sense of uncertainty. He trusted all he needed to appear at the right time.

I must learn to practice the wise ways of the frog by trusting that what I need will show up when I am ready.

Little Toy Soldiers

Maybe it was talking about dreams and their meaning with someone yesterday. Or perhaps it was reality inserting itself.

But it was a dream straight out of last year's events: the past meeting the present with its people and even projects from another time marching back into the present. Each demanded to appear before me to convince me of their importance in my life. Like the queen in Alice in Wonderland, each appeared before me to be heard, not one at a time but all at once. They lined up like perfectly dressed toy soldiers, not the mismatched fairy tale characters of the story. They were ready to battle to return to their place in my life, or at least in my memory. Then there is a loud noise, and they all scatter.

"Wait. Come back. I need to know what happened," I cried.

Sleep fades as I turn off the alarm, remembering that was a dream, not reality. It was a reality dream. As I breathe deep, calming yoga breaths, it isn't the people or the events I remember. Instead, it is the long-forgotten feelings buried in a life that moved on, demanding time in my presence, feelings that want to know and understand what happened.

But reality inserts itself again, reminding me this is a work-day insisting on attention. I vow to do something with it that makes more sense than that dream.

This Is My Song

My mornings generally begin on the deck, observing and listening to the sounds of the forest waking up. It isn't often, however, that I can quiet my mind long enough to become part of the morning.

As I ventured out today, a light fog was already forming over the river. The air was still and felt heavy from the fog's weight. As often happens when it's like that, it creeps up the hillside through the trees until it reaches the edges of the deck, where it paused as if someone suddenly raised a big red stop sign. I especially like the times when the fog comes onto the deck and includes me in its journey, but that was not to be today.

This time, it began retreating into the trees, which must have been an alarm clock for the birds hiding there because their morning songs started, one by one. The small birds sing first, and others join in until joyful expressions spread over the river, waking the larger fowl along the water's edge.

There are so many different calls it is difficult to distinguish one from the other, but the distinct piercing call of a red-tailed hawk allows my ears to focus. Listening in this way allowed me to experience the sensation of oneness with the fog, the forest, and the river.

It was a mystical moment that only lasted a few minutes, but memories of other times I have felt this connection awakened within me. It has been a while since I was still long enough in the early morning to allow the noise of my to-do list to lose its relevance and the music of this miracle's divine source to come through. All that was missing now was to have a song of my own so I could join in the bird chorus. Then I realized this is my song.

Painting at Dawn

Watching dawn break through a veil of leaves is like slowly lifting the drape from a painting in progress. As the sky grows lighter, the distant ridges and the river slowly start to appear, forming distinct lines that define where one ends and the other begins. The Painter's tentative brush of muted colors suddenly becomes bold and daring and, though distinctly separate, reveals the connectedness of sky, land, and water. The warm summer air I breathe is the same air that wafts over this magical landscape, pulling me into the scene so that I become part of this magical view.

It is the feeling of connectedness with all things that brings deep inner knowing that with the dawn, we can begin again with the blank canvas of the new day before us. Paint whatever you want there and make it a masterpiece.

Let the Mystery Unfold

As I watch the sunrise coloring the river in shades of red and orange, I know with certainty there is a path I'm supposed to follow. I can see the well-lit path of the sun on the water, but the one I travel is a mystery. I know I must walk it and that I have to let the ambiguity of it unfold. There is no guide or navigational system to direct me on when to turn or which way to go. My heart and soul know the way, but they are not talking except to vaguely whisper trust us.

The flow of life is similar to the water in the river. It is deep, even at the shoreline making it impossible to see its depth. All I can do is trust that my heart and soul know the way, so I must follow their lead and have faith that my feet stay on the path.

The Catch in Change

Change: some fear it; some embrace it and some accept it once time has allowed for processing what's involved. But we all experience it many times throughout our lives. Self-help gurus have written volumes on the topic, yet we still struggle with acceptance even though we understand the necessity of it.

Today, a friend and I had an intensely focused discussion on the process of making changes, including how one decides if and when it is needed. We didn't have much time to talk as we each had previous commitments waiting, but we reached a mutual conclusion that there are three types of change.

There is change that is totally out of our control, such as job loss, death, or natural devastation. We must accept that action is required, or we lose control of our lives if we don't.

Then, there is change forced on us by alterations in the lives of others; we agreed this situation is mostly relationship concerns. Sometimes, we have choices in these situations; sometimes we don't.

But as we talked, we agreed that the most challenging adjustments are those that would improve our lives once we get beyond the disarray of it. In most cases, the change would make life better for everyone involved. Then why is this so difficult?

There were no concrete conclusions to our musings, yet the conversation and my subsequent thoughts about it on the drive home profoundly disturbed my tranquility. In the first scenario, I can quickly make order from chaos, which starts to present calm. The second scenario requires negotiation with the parties involved and has differences unique to each situation that must be considered.

But, it is the third one, a change that would make life better for me, that I agonize over. I must analyze it, take it apart, and put it back together so many times that I lose myself in the maze I create. As I process this newly found insight, I hope that in the future I allow myself permission to rearrange whatever needs to be modified without interference from my overthinking.

Inside a Snow Globe

The snow plow was fighting a losing battle. I watched in wonder and amusement as it passed by, headed south on my street, and again as it made the return trip in the northbound lane. This happened twice, and still, the snow kept accumulating.

The scene I am observing from my window is like a globe that one gives a hearty shake to watch the snowflakes swirl around encapsulated images within a tiny magical world. We cannot resist one more shake to activate the fairytale captured within that glass world.

The street scene before me is that the swirling wonderland of white flakes that covers the road faster than the snow plow can clear it. However, it is not likely amusing to the driver, who eventually quit plowing. I am watching from behind the glass of my window while the elements give another shake to create a swirl of white one more time.

As I continue to watch, I wonder if I am part of some fantasy, a miniature creature trapped in a scene from which I cannot escape and I am being rearranged to create new energy in my life.

From My Heart to Yours

Evenings on the river are lovely and serene. The golden glow of late-day sunlight on the water, the symphony created by the songs of the night birds and bugs, the chirping of the squirrels, and the powerful, thundering buzz from tiny hummingbird wings combine to entice me to linger a while and absorb it all.

The sky, streaked with thin, white clouds with frayed edges, is much like yarn handled often but with no pattern yet to hint at what it will become. A lone boat makes its way somewhere else, breaking the spell with its noise.

This piece of earth that I call mine soothes my weary soul and inspires me to keep writing. When finished, I shall scatter my words on the water with wishes that they find their way to your heart.

Let There Be Light

Be the Light

There is an unusual stillness in the morning air, even though the leaves hanging over the deck move ever so slightly.

Across the river, a thin veil of fog is forming, rising upward from the water. I listened for the usual birdsong, but the sounds I heard were muted and coming from deeper in the forest. I am thinking about the music convention where I had planned to be this week and remembering past years there. Melodies from so many guitars wrap around you, much like the fog that has now climbed the riverbank and upward through the trees, draping everything in its soft mist.

I sip the warm coffee from the cup in my hand as I recall writing in early January about my intention to do things differently this year. At the time, I thought I was writing only about my plans for the year, but as I reread it, I realized the insight in those shared words came from a place of deep knowing that change would affect life far beyond mine.

As the fog around the deck lifts, the morning sun fills the space with light. Sometimes we allow our minds to get trapped in darkness, turning our thoughts inward and forgetting to look toward the light on the horizon. Our actions can become based on those dark thoughts, and we subsequently spread them around us. Yet, if we lift our heads and look in the direction of the light, it beckons us to move in that direction.

We choose to be a source of light or darkness with every word we say and every action we take. Like the fog dissipating in the sunlight, darkness disappears when light is present. I say a silent prayer that I will always have the courage to hold out a light to help penetrate the darkness.

Courage Is a Light

It takes courage to not only examine your truth but also to live it. You have to be unafraid of breaking the outer shell that covers the things you fear. When you do, you find the beauty of your naked beliefs in the broken pieces of what you once embraced as rock-solid. Then, when you attain the confidence to live what you believe, you must reach deep into the well of courage again.

Change in yourself often creates ripples of discomfort for those who wish you to remain as you were, especially when it becomes necessary to establish a boundary. Boundaries preserve relationships so that each individual can grow at their own pace.

Courage takes compassion and understanding as you allow space for others to be who they are. It is a light you shine that others can follow.

If Only I Could Fly

for Joe Long

It's four in the morning, and I should be sleeping. Instead, I am standing barefoot on the cold, frosty wood of the deck, bathed in the moon's white light.

I watched from this same spot last evening as the moon peeked tentatively over the ridgeline across the river as if uncertain whether to make the ascent into the night sky.

And then, after the seeming hesitation, there it was, full and golden, climbing upward and casting its light across the water. There were pools of it in places, making the water appear lit from underneath its dark surface. But, the long, shimmering beam it cast toward me ignited my imagination.

I imagined walking into that beam, following it across the water, and climbing it upward until I was inside that golden sphere of light. As I became part of the moon, we traveled across the sky, spreading beams to light the land for those in the darkness below. I imagined how it would feel to ride inside the moon until I could descend on a beam of light, landing quietly beside you, where you are gazing upward into your sky. I imagined I was back in the place I stood before you went away, where we stood together under the same moon, imagining infinitely golden possibilities.

But it's four in the morning, and the cold wood beneath my feet snaps me back to reality. The golden moonbeams of last night have turned into a white light that now feels as cold as the night itself.

I watch as the moon moves away from me, descending from sight behind the ridges, taking its light and leaving me with only my imagination and cold feet.

Divine Presence

Sometimes just before dawn, the river catches light from a source I cannot see. It is as if the water is light, with the surface reflecting the surrounding landscape like a mirror. My eyes search the dark sky for an explanation, but I find only a covering of gray clouds.

I stand mesmerized, taking in the mystery to fill my senses with the quiet beauty that is a miracle of the night. I hear a whisper deep within that reminds me the Source of Light is always with me, whether I acknowledge its presence or not.

Light in the Dark

As often happens when the moon is nearing its full phase, I am pulled awake by the light that seeps through the blinds at four in the morning. This morning was no exception to that mysterious happening.

But the pull does not stop with awakening me. It does not stop until I am outside, on the deck, soaking up the moonlight and gazing at the starlit sky above me. This morning, the moon is low in the western sky. A shaft of moonlight beams through the trees until it reaches me.

I find myself thinking about my writing that I have temporarily abandoned because I felt criticized for the rawness of my expression. I write from the heart and the futility of trying to change that will alter the reality of the feeling.

As I shivered in the night air, I knew that I could no more change who I am or what wants to be expressed through me than the moon can change its light.

So, I shall pick up my pen and begin again, and may the words I write be the light you need when the path becomes dark.

When Planets Align

Mornings are a miraculous and joyful time of day. One can see the miracle in the space between the fading night and day beginning. The moon setting behind the ridges in the west casts a silvery light across the deck and landscape, but it does not diminish the beginning glow of dawn from the east. The two create luminosity in the river, making the water look like liquid silver. Overhead, the deep blue sky displays stars and planets that sparkle through the branches of the old trees, their tops now so far above me that the part of the sky I can see has become smaller.

I watched this exchange of dark and light, moon and sun, from the warm side of the window, my face so close to the glass I could feel the cold from the other side. As I scanned the heavens hoping to see the five planets aligned there, a brilliant shooting star streaked across my small sky, too fast for me to make a wish on it. So, I wished for another star.

As the sun moved higher in the sky, the difference of night and day was similar to the contrast between ridges and water. I used to see this splendor only if everything in my life felt perfect. But I discovered that I do not have to deny myself the joy in life because I am also experiencing its pain. There is always beauty in the ordinary.

I wish these miracles of contrast and alignment for you as you experience each new day.

The Long Darkness

It is three in the morning and I am fully awake. I went outside in the cold to soak up the beauty of the night sky. The moon is not visible, but the heavens twinkle with millions of stars that adorn the heavens with their brilliance.

I walk cautiously around the deck, holding onto chair backs as I look up, making my way around its expanse to view the sky from every angle visible within this space. It is quiet at this time of night. In the moonlight, the river looks like liquid glass as if it has consumed the silver light from above.

The quiet is interrupted when I step on a stray acorn, sending a sharp explosion of sound through the calm, and then bump into a wind chime, the one that has stanzas from Amazing Grace printed on the pipes. The soft sweet sounds become part of the night's mystery.

I am deliberately up at this time of night because I want to fully experience this part of the day leading into the longest night of the year, a time of the long darkness that marks the return of the light.

I pause in my attempt to look up as I walk for fear of creating more noise. My stillness causes the cold to penetrate both consciousness and clothing, so I retreat to the warmth inside.

I have just returned from visiting with friends in another city. Our celebration of friendship and our shared love of music renewed my spirit and soul. It was a perfect time for honoring the light offered by this gift of human connection.

Winter Solstice is my favorite day of the year, and I spend much of the day in quiet reflection. When darkness falls later today, I will honor the day by lighting candles and offering a gratitude prayer for all the special people who bring light to my life in the way stars decorate the night sky.

Window of Hope

Watching the sky at sunrise is like beginning each day with a new miracle and renewed hope.

The sky is almost solid cloud cover this morning, but a tiny hole has appeared, a beam of light from Venus drilling through the denseness. But clouds took over again, covering the light. As I watched and waited, other openings began to appear. One took the shape of a window and grew bigger, allowing more sunlight to emerge. To the left, the formations are like trees or oddly-shaped buildings. By the time the sun became visible, the cloud formations had disbanded and scattered, making way for the clarity of daylight.

Life is that way much of the time. Sometimes, our lives become cloudy with challenges, and we do not see a solution. Then a tiny, bright spot appears, offering hope as the light shines through and we see more clearly. We can then navigate through another of life's cloudy pathways. The days of our lives are composed of these tiny miracles of light that appear when we most need them, lighting our pathways with hope.

Source of My Strength

The week behind me presented many challenges that required immediate attention and daily action, leaving little time for my morning reflection. So, I took extra time this morning to allow my soul to breathe.

Wrapped in a blanket, I sat in the chill of the fading night to watch the miracle above me as the meteor shower ended. A long, thin layer of wispy clouds spread over the starlit sky at first, but these soon dissolved, and all I could see was sky and stars. And trees; they are always within my vision and have become so tall now that they lean in toward each other at their tops as if in conversation. Their steadfastness whispers to me, reminding me of my strength and the Source of it.

A few remaining meteoroids flamed and streaked downward, rewarding my patience. As I watched the stars fade in the dawning of the day, I became aware that my heart rate and breathing had slowed, leaving me in calm oneness with all that was happening around me. I thought of how easy it is to allow ourselves to get caught up in the have-to-do lists of life and forget that light for our path is always there. Sometimes it may be only for the next step, yet it is always present. But we have to look up to see it. Guidance for our path comes from looking to the Source and trusting that we will always have what we need to illuminate our way in meeting life's challenges.

Time to Go

One of the first signs that summer is ready to make way for fall is the appearance of gaping holes in the curtain of leaves that have hidden my view of the river and ridges for months. A few leaves have fallen but many are shrinking as if their tree has quietly whispered, "Wrap it up. It's getting late, and you've got to go."

The golden glow in the spaces between the leaves reminds me that the Divine Source of Light is always there, guiding my walk through challenges and triumphs alike. In the same way, the leaves inherently prepare to change their colors. I sense it is safe to breathe, for I am never left alone in my life's walk, and there is always light in the spaces between.

Return of the Light

It is still dark as many are beginning their day. I've been writing since before dawn and needed a break, so I went outside to feel the chill of the soggy nighttime.

The winter solstice is my favorite day of the year, despite the darkness or maybe because of it. The arrival of this day means that tomorrow the light begins its return. It is barely noticeable to most, but it is still a turning point, filled with the hope and promises that light always brings.

The warmth from the cup of coffee in my hands is in stark contrast to the chill in the air as I linger in the early dawn, thinking of how different this morning was from the dawn of last year's Winter Solstice when my heart was still heavy from family tragedy and grief.

Thus, our days pass us by, marked by moments and memories that we treasure or events that bring us pain. We either thrive or wither in those spaces between the dark and light of our lives, yet we measure time by years gone by rather than moments that make us feel alive.

I silently vow to hold on to and treasure those moments of love and light.

Now Is All There Is

Flight Home

The eagle was flying upriver, headed home in the silvery light of an almost full moon over water smooth as glass, beautifully punctuating the end of a perfect day. I watched, mesmerized by the spectacular beauty of the scene.

My first thought at witnessing this magical moment was to grab my camera and capture the scene in a photo. But the wisdom within spoke softly and profoundly, "Let yourself just experience this magnificence so that its beauty settles in your soul." I chose to listen to the small voice.

The eagle is back this morning, fishing along the riverbank, and I am grateful for experiencing the lesson he offered that brought me home to the present moment.

All in Good Time

So many times, I have sat in the dark in this same spot on the deck feeling rather than seeing the magic as night turns to day, but it never gets old. There is always some new sensation to experience.

This time I sit poised with my stargazing binoculars, hoping the clouds will move on to some other part of the sky. After all, it's not like I am greedy. I am not asking to see the entire sky; I want only to view a small part of it for now.

As if reading my thoughts, the clouds floating in groups have banded together and then spread themselves across my field of view like one smooths brownie batter in the baking pan. I've never seen them do that before. It's as if they want to tell me, "All in good time; all in good time."

Not yet ready to abandon my hope of seeing a star, I put the binoculars down and rest my head on the back of the chair as I scan the sky above for a break in the clouds. I feel what I think is a raindrop, although rain was not in the forecast. Then another one lands on the other cheek, and I wonder how often these tiny raindrops fall, and I don't see or feel them. Am I missing the magic of my life because I am always in motion?

Silent moments like this provide rest for another day and a busy week looming ahead. I put the binoculars away and give in to the soothing sensation of the stray raindrops as I listen to the silence surrounding me.

Leaning In

There are moments during the summer months and in storms with high winds when I think about clearing some of the trees from around the house. Storms cause a safety concern because trees might fall on the house if uprooted by the wind. But cutting them to have a better view of the sky, the river, and the ridges during the spring and summer months is not something my mind or my heart can justify.

As I was contemplating the idea, the trees came alive with activity. The birds who live in those trees would survive. They can fly, but the squirrels would have a transportation problem. They use the branches to travel from tree to tree the way we use the interstate system to get from one place to another.

And then there is the way the trees lean in toward each other as if in conversation, sometimes including me in their discussion when I get quiet enough to hear. Leaning into the wind is how they survive storms. The thought of leaning in suggests that I need to do that with my life, lean into it instead of holding back.

I must trust my inner knowing that all is well when it storms. The trees offer life lessons in remaining flexible as they sway and bend; even the creatures that use them as shelter and playground know this secret. I know I will let the trees stand as I watch a squirrel leap upward to a higher branch on his way to the neighboring tree showing me what it means to lean into each new day.

Morning Music

The air feels colder than the 57-degree reading on the thermometer and the breeze is strong enough to set the wind spinners in motion. It's the beginning of Memorial Day weekend, and the river will become filled with the noise from boats full of people enjoying life but disturbing the quiet of this serene place.

At the moment, all I hear are the birds of the forest and river singing their morning songs to greet the day. As I write, a hummingbird appears, hovering to offer a soft chirp as if to say hello. Then, he flies to the feeder with a roar of wings and returns to buzz my head, perhaps telling me I am blocking his flight path to the feeder.

My attention turns to the trees around me and how tall they are now. Most are oaks with deep roots that drink from the river. In the distance, I hear a pileated woodpecker at work on a metal tower. That happens often, and I wonder if the sound resonates inside his head. Closer to me, I hear a smaller one softly tapping on a tree. From the river, the geese and great blue herons are waking up, and their honks and squawks are harsh against the soft songs of the smaller birds.

The sun has risen, casting a long shaft of golden light across the water, reminding me that I am cold. I shiver and decide to go back inside. I will keep the morning music in my heart to remind me how it will be again after the weekend noise recedes.

Seasons of Life

My intention for my early morning time had been to sit quietly in my reading chair and watch the sunrise break over the ridges. Yet, I couldn't resist peeking out the window, which changed everything. The leaves are swaying as if dancing to their favorite song. Daylight was breaking through the ever-widening spaces between the leaves on the old trees as the wind claimed the brown ones. I know from many years of observing these signs that the temperature will be cold this morning. Finally, I gave in and moved to the deck to watch the day unfold. That feeling in the air created an excitement that only the beginning of fall can bring to my summer-weary soul.

Fall is my favorite time of year, and the colors of the season renew my spirit and fill me with joy, but this morning I am overwhelmed by melancholy. Like summer eventually ends, the glorious fall weather will also end soon. Like life, the end is the beginning, and the beginning will become another end, even as I long for fall to stay a while longer.

A hummingbird appeared, hesitated, and then stopped to examine me. He sounds so loud as his tiny wings rotate in fast motion to keep him suspended in place. When satisfied that I am harmless, he lands on the feeder, drinking his fill of the sweet nectar. He returns to make a complete circle around me at eye level before heading out to wake the others.

There are many life lessons in nature. The one at the heart of my morning reflection is endings. While I reflect on the loss, hummingbirds do not have such thoughts. They go about their routine of living their purpose and finding the places that hold their life-giving nectar. Likewise, the leaves that whisper as they allow the breeze to sway them to and fro do not attempt to remain rigid and unmovable; instead, they surrender to the music, which will cease in a few weeks. They won't grieve the loss of the music. They will take their cue and let go of what's finished as they join other leaves that have already fallen, where they nourish the tree in the spring.

Waiting

I sat in silence as the sun rose over the distant ridges, and the sky turned from gray to golden, then red, finally giving way to copper. I wanted to hear what the silence had to tell me.

But this morning, there were no profound insights, no ah-ha moments, no inspirational messages hanging in the air to be plucked like ripe fruit and placed into the basket of my waiting soul.

The usual morning sounds were missing, except those coming from the nearby nest that contained the chattering juvenile ospreys that had yet to take their first flight. What were they waiting for? They should have left the nest days ago. Were they waiting for the perfect moment to try something new? Or maybe they were waiting for a breeze so they could leap into the air current and ride without effort.

As I listened to their conversational-like sounds, realization dawned in the same way that the colors of the morning sky had subtly unfolded. I looked at the planner beside me and shuddered at the long to-do list. There were so many things I still wanted to do with my life that had nothing to do with the to-do list that only lulled me into the appearance of accomplishing something. My plans and goals include traveling, writing a book, and watching the sunrise in Taos. Why did my to-do list have mundane entries like picking up dry cleaning and buying new nail polish? These things must be done but do not further my life goals.

Perhaps there was a message in my interpretation of the ospreys' delay in leaving the nest after all.

What am I waiting for to jump into the things I dream of?

Wisdom of the Deck Squirrel

Yesterday was one of those days that began with a slow, soothing rain that was both mellow and inspiring. By day's end, the rain poured from the sky as if to punish the dry earth with its intensity, turning the easygoing feeling into soupy dreariness.

Today is a different experience. Nothing is dreary out my window as the sun blankets everything in light, and the only grayness is the bare trees and the deck squirrel. I watch him as he zips about, pausing to nibble on some tasty morsel that distracts him, momentarily slowing him down.

Does he know how beautiful he is against the background of the coppery-colored leaves of fall and the blue of the river in the background? Does he know I watch him through the window while he lives as if this moment is all there is? Does he measure the passing of days by how many full moons have come and gone this year?

I watch as he chases about joyfully, oblivious that a human is just a few feet away, writing about him and the lesson he wants to teach her about living. As I muse about what he might tell me, I'm sure I heard him whisper that I am overthinking and should come out on the deck and play while the sun shines.

Personally Speaking

Mining for Truth at Chimney Rock

Sometimes we go in search of what was lost, or maybe we just want closure. This was what I hoped to do when I embarked on a three-week vacation in Colorado to determine whether a resolution was possible for a broken relationship. We had met on a backpacking trip in the Colorado Mountains while I was in college. If I returned to the place of that magical time in my life, I hoped I could at least develop an understanding of what went wrong and where.

Chimney Rock was a place I had seen from a distance on previous trips, and I hoped to hike it on this vacation. This place was sacred to people from long ago and is now a preserved national monument. Thus protected, treks to the top are by guided tour only.

Purify all that you touch, purify that which is in you is a Pueblo song quoted on a marker at the ranger station, and it seemed to foretell what I would sense at the top. The hike was paused only for breathing breaks, making the experience at the top more meaningful and the view spectacular. The tour guide gave his presentation and then permitted the group to explore and enjoy the view. I walked away for a quiet moment of reflection, but I was unprepared for what happened next.

The energy of the place was so powerful that I was unaware of breathing or even of being. It was a feeling of oneness with the site's energy and the earth, wind, and sky. A ray of sunlight appeared directly in front of me and wanted me to pay attention to that moment and that spot and what the sun saw that I could not.

After I could breathe again, I returned to where the guide stood alone and realized he was as profoundly moved as I was. The remnants of housing and daily living of these ancient people are evident along the way to the top. Still, the most magnificent one was at the peak, where the spiritual leaders held ceremonies. We talked in low reverent voices about the power of the place as we sensed the presence and reason the pinnacle had been reserved for spiritual traditions. The effect on both of us was so profound that tears flowed slowly and silently down our cheeks as we talked.

While the experience was extraordinary, it was on the way down that one of the most powerful insights I have experienced occurred. It is human nature to want to protect ourselves from emotional pain, but at some point, we must dig deeper to excavate the treasure inside. It takes great courage to go mining for the truth within. You have to be unafraid of breaking the outer shell that has covered the things you fear. But when you do, you find the beauty of your naked truth is in the shards of the brokenness within, not in the decorative exterior you painted to please the eyes of others. Such insightful experiences become treasures like the shards of pottery from ancient sites like this one.

One has only to stand at the summit of this place to feel the energy from long ago. I began the trek to the top to take in the views and see the ceremonial location of ancient spiritual leaders. But I experienced the spirit of the site in a deep way that was to determine the direction of my life from that moment forward. I did not reach closure on that trip, but I discovered what I had lost. It was me. It was that moment I took my power back and began to live in my newly found truth.

Breakthrough at Blue River

For most of my life, I have struggled to understand why something happened the way it did, especially the causes of broken relationships. But while on vacation in Colorado, I experienced multiple insights with subsequent breakthroughs in releasing the need to understand before letting go.

On a peaceful afternoon following a challenging hike, I experienced one of the most profound insights of my life as I watched the water flow in a small stream that ran close to the cabin. The water flowed freely in most of the stream, but a clump of small foliage formed a blockage in one place, restricting the straight-line movement. The force of the water eventually broke through the clog and went around it.

As I watched this happen multiple times, I sensed a deep comprehension of a blockage in the current of my life. I had been reflecting on life's twists and turns and the recent unraveling of a personal relationship as I listened to the calming bubble and gurgle of water over stones. Suddenly, I understood it was not necessary to identify why something happened the way it did. Instead, one has only to accept that it happened to free the heart and soul to move the same way the stream flows to join the Blue River.

While painful, had it not been for my broken heart, I would not have been sitting in peace enjoying the soul-soothing music of this small stream. I accepted with deep gratitude the necessity of going through heartbreak to allow my life to flow freely again, moving me along when I could not do that on my own.

In that moment of quiet reflection, I accepted that I no longer needed to understand why events happened; I had only to acknowledge that they did. I dropped the need to know into that small stream and left it there, allowing the water to carry it away.

Embracing the Fear

As I headed out for an early walk, the air felt heavy with moisture. I was distracted by thoughts of things I needed to do, so I was only partially present in this activity. Suddenly, a young buck watching my approach leaped into the air and ran down the hill away from me. He stopped in a clearing where he was more visible now than when surrounded by trees. The noise startled me, yanking me back into the moment and awareness of my surroundings. I thought about the deer's flight for the remainder of my walk.

We often run away from our safe place directly into situations that leave us vulnerable and exposed like that young deer when he fled from the shadows into the light. Why do we run, especially when it is safer to stay?

I thought of times I had felt tempted to run from painful situations but somehow found the courage to stand and face whatever emotion had frightened me. As I thought about those past situations, I realized that while I didn't run, I had moved out of the shadows into the light as I permitted myself to feel and embrace my fear, often returning to where I began with renewed strength.

That could be what the young buck experienced this morning, running from a perceived threat into a position to assess the danger. He returned to foraging for breakfast, concluding there was no threat. I finished my walk and returned to the safety of my sunroom, free of the distractions that had threatened my peaceful morning.

Finding Peace Within the Noise

The summer storms have been unrelenting, and the high winds accompanying them take down the trees, breaking the power lines. When this happens during the day, there is enough light that I can remain productive. But the outage lasted well into the night, finally forcing me to surrender to the darkness. Even reading with the book light became impossible. Its tiny glow was no match for the darkness of the night.

So, I reluctantly gave in, lit the candles, and allowed the tranquility of the night's silence to wash over me. As my mind became calm, I realized how far away I had drifted from my practice of quiet time. I had allowed the world's noise to creep into my space and disrupt my peace. This insight was jolting. How could I have become so busy that I had no time for quiet reflection?

As the light of the candles danced and swayed on the table in front of me, I vowed to become more diligent in guarding against allowing the noise of life to rob me of the very thing that gives me the courage to face it. I must allocate time and create space so that peace can return to my soul.

The world's noise will continue, but I do not have to let it darken my life. Storms of nature and those of life come and go, and world events will sometimes create anxiety. But if I retain stillness within, I do not have to let these events become another stress. Connecting to that still place within allows me to disregard the noise and remain peaceful.

Holy Dirt

There is a room in the chapel at Chimayo in Northern New Mexico believed to contain Holy Dirt which is said to have healing properties. I visited the chapel today and spent time in that room, allowing the tears of my grief to flow freely. I have recently chosen to be deliberately detached and quiet, and this sacred place was a pause between my past and future.

As I reflect on what's next, I wonder how many times one can start over in our short life on earth. And then, as clearly as if it had come from someone sitting beside me, I heard, "As many times as it takes to fulfill your purpose."

Recently, a friend wanted to engage in a philosophical debate. The intention was well-meaning; however, I cannot allow myself to engage in anything resembling conflict if I am to fulfill my purpose. Like most, I've had my share of personal and professional politics to deal with in my career, and I've managed to navigate most of it quite well. There is no place for that in this next phase of my life. I will continue giving freely from my heart as I always have, but I must focus on maintaining peace within.

Time away on vacation solidified this deep knowing that I must maintain the sacredness of my space.

Moving Beyond Pain

My early morning quiet time was shattered this morning by tears that my steeliness seldom allows, but today, they escaped uncontrollably from eyes that saw life through words written long ago and then forgotten. They were lyrical words from a life rich with experiences that created a profound understanding rivaling that of any modern-day self-help guru. Yet, they were words from an old soul who has felt too much, sharing her laughter along the way but saving up her tears like storing water in a well for use in a drought.

The tears escaped this morning to soothe the pain: the pain of the little girl who never got to be a child, the pain in the heart of the woman who realizes her life is composed of more yesterdays than tomorrows, and the pain from the weariness of a broken spirit that craves respite for her soul.

But it is through my writing that I have uncovered the wisdom hidden deep within, and it is my writing that brushes away the tears, knowing that I will continue to be just who I am and will go on holding the light for those who walk an unlit path. I will, however, start sharing those words so I no longer have to carry the experiences alone.

Reflections on Living in a Forest

The view from the deck is my gauge for seasonal changes, especially the arrival of fall. At first, the only indication that change is imminent is the shrinking of the leaves. The sparseness opens up more spaces, allowing a better view of the sky and the terrain beyond the river. Gradually, the leaves began to turn yellow and red, the latter showing up first.

Yesterday, just before dawn, I sat in my favorite spot and watched night fade as the sun assumed control of the sky and lit up the forest. Dawn is a perfect time of day to be still and listen. Sometimes, I listen to my inner self, but at other times, I listen to the messages of the trees and the creatures that inhabit them.

It was reassuring to hear acorns dropping from the trees. It is a long way to the ground. These old trees are at least 100 feet tall, so the falling acorns land with a thud or a crash, depending on whether they hit the soft earth or the hard surface of the neighbor's roof. Last year, there were no acorns, which meant food was scarce for the squirrels and deer that live here.

However, the breeze is fierce this morning, a predictor of how the hurricane on the coast will affect weather this far inland. Instead of falling straight down, the acorns are like missiles today as the approaching storm sends them flying onto my deck this time, and way too close to my head for me to fully appreciate that the forest creatures will have food for the winter.

As the wind speed intensified, I retreated to the safety of the sunroom, where I could continue my musings without feeling the need for a helmet. From here, all appears to be quiet as the leaves suddenly become motionless.

Abandoning my vigil on the deck is rewarded with another magical moment of living in a forest. My heart smiles as the resident red fox makes her morning rounds, circling the house looking for breakfast or patrolling to ensure her territory has remained intact.

Living in this place provides daily opportunities for reflection where the meaning of life and the Divine Order of Things is always visible. Thus, I begin my day with deep gratitude, knowing that life goes on and it is good.

The Weight I Carry

The fog is so heavy this morning that its weight sounds like a soft rain as it makes contact with the leaves of the oak trees. There are no other sounds except the thud of falling acorns. I have chosen a spot on the deck away from the house to avoid being hit by acorns. But even as I have the thought, a huge one hits the roof of the house again and is propelled upward, landing behind my chair as if to say I can find you. I pick up the fog-soaked acorn, feeling its damp weight.

My mood turns somber, and I feel the weight of world events related to the pandemic pierce my thoughts, dampen my spirit, and settle in my soul. For one who never faces a problem without seeing solutions, this is an unfamiliar place to be, for this is not one I'm in charge of solving. However, I am responsible for actions I take that might affect others. Each individual's activity contributes to the well-being of, or damage to, the whole. Like the pop of the falling acorn warning that I might get hit, there are signs in most events that offer options for resolution.

While our individual lives may be good, we sometimes become complacent and out of touch with what is happening around us. Then something transpires that gets our attention, and we become concerned. But just as knowing that dense fog is not rain, we must learn to discern the gravity of each situation, solve what we can, and then put down what's not ours to carry.

Don't Weep for Me

The rose-colored sunrise creates stripes like a horizontal candy cane across the sky. I'm drawn to the window to look closer, but that's not enough. I find myself outside in my pajamas with bare feet as if pulled through the glass.

I had not planned to start the day yanked out of my half-asleep state. I'm sitting beneath the hummingbird feeder, trying not to move because this tiny winged bit of joy has come for breakfast. I'm here to watch the sunrise, yet she is part of the sunrise, a participant, not a spectator.

My thoughts drifted toward yesterday's conversation with a friend about my lifelong role of always being in a problem-solving mode. This habit learned early in life trained my brain to begin formulating work-around strategies at the first hint of something going wrong. She pointed out that the situation we were discussing didn't call for problem-solving. Instead, I should experience the day as it unfolds. She suggested that, in this case, I could think of possibilities and what-if miracles instead of going into battle mode. I should even consider celebrating.

 A wren suddenly lights on the deck railing, singing her song of hope, looking straight at me as if she wants to remind me that I've lost a part of me. The crows agreed as they caw-cawed from the trees. My friend's admonishments vibrate within my being, and I feel my soul weep for the load I've carried for others all these years. I know I've done what's right, but it's time for me to turn that compassion upon myself and allow the door of possibilities to open for me.

Truth under the Fog

The dawn on this last day of the year is evident as the last glow of moonlight faintly lights the sky.

But even as I write these words, fog forms over the river. Soon it will creep upward and outward to blanket the old trees standing watch along the water. In the summertime, their leaves shield me from seeing what is happening on the river, but now they stand leafless and bare, exposing beauty not usually visible when fully leafed-out.

That is how this year has evolved, as we have faced reality in a way never before encountered as a result of the pandemic. Today, many will be relieved that this year is over. Endings and beginnings are not as simple as hanging a new wall calendar or making the first entry in a new planner.

Life-changes closely resemble an ombre-patterned fabric, where colors subtly change from one shade to another. As tomorrow dawns and we begin a new year, we will make well-meaning resolutions and express gratitude that this year is behind us.

As we look back, the year-end serves as a mirror that reflects whatever is in front of it. The mirror cannot change what it reflects. That is Truth. Change comes from intentional action, not from turning the calendar pages. The fog that covered the view of the river this morning did not make the river disappear. The water still exists and flows under the mist. These are examples of truths that do not change.

To arrive at Truth, we must step into the light to see and know it and then have the courage to accept and live it. This was a life-changing understanding for me as I turn the page of my new calendar.

Untying the Knots

My practice of beginning my day in silence as the dark turns to light always offers new perspectives on life.

This morning I noticed lights dancing about in the trees closest to me and those across the river. My first thought was of fireflies, but it's too cool and too late in the year for these tiny light sources to fly about, especially at four-thirty in the morning. I wanted to go outside to investigate but was too comfortable to make an effort.

As I continued to watch the unusual dancing lights display, I realized that it was wind causing this early morning spectacle that made the lights appear, then disappear, only to pop up again in a different place. Having solved this mystery, my mind wandered freely through recent family situations and the few remaining issues that needed final resolution.

As often happens with untethered thoughts, they float from one issue to another searching for a connection. It occurred to me that insight often reveals itself, like the wind made the lights appear and disappear. Just like the lights across the river bobbed and weaved through the spaces in the wind-blown trees, our understanding appears in small increments that open our minds to solutions for only the portion of the problem that needs solving now. A complex problem can only be solved in stages, especially those involving others, so we have insight only for each step in the process, not the entire solution.

I ventured outside to find the wind was fierce, and the brown leaves fell like the rain I hadn't expected. Life's storms are necessary to shake loose those aspects that have served their purpose. Losing that which is no longer helpful allows light to flood the shadows, thus exposing painful truths that need resolution.

It is comforting to know that in my silence, I can hear the wisdom in my soul that always guides me when it is time to untie the knots in my life.

Vulnerability of the Journey

The contrast of light and dark on the river creates a mysterious appearance to the landscape this morning. Most leaves have fallen from the oaks along the shoreline. As much as I enjoy the view, I feel vulnerable and exposed when the trees around me are bare.

The morning light has changed as I write, and the river has become a silvery thread of water that, despite its appearance of standing still, is moving toward the ocean, not knowing what that journey holds. But it continues to flow toward its destiny without appearing to feel susceptible to treacherous blockages to its progress along the way.

When I feel vulnerable, I am inclined to suppress the thoughts that caused it because accepting the vulnerability of my deepest feelings requires equal courage. To grow, I must learn to stand unafraid when my instinct is to cover or deny the source of my discomfort.

For months, I felt protected from the elements by the shielding from the green serenity of the trees. A few weeks later, fall's fiery color ignites every fiber of my being, so I forget what is ahead for the trees. The red and gold leaves become brown, temperatures drop, and the wind strips the trees, leaving them naked. Maybe my vulnerability reflects the trees' experience when stripped of their covering, leaving their bare branches visible and unprotected.

What I Tell Myself

A life philosophy I subscribed to years ago included refusal to wear a label placed on me by someone else, including parents, teachers, managers, spiritual leaders, and doctors. As I watched others become broken by what someone called them, I silently vowed to never allow that to happen to me. Ironically, I was surprised to realize the person I had to be most mindful of doing this was me. If we mentally refer to ourselves as something demeaning, we may believe it to be true.

We must be constantly aware of our self-talk. It does not matter what others call me. I ignore it, but what I call myself can make or break me. What I call myself can make me well or bring me to my knees in pain. What I tell myself can make me happy, healthy, and whole or cause me to become depressed, sick, or grow old prematurely.

This awareness brought profound clarity, just like sunlight erases the shadows of the night. I had been beating myself up over someone else's perception of what my life should be.

The most important aspect is that what I tell myself creates my perception of life. It was an eye opening moment the day I realized how important it is to be mindful of how I talk to me.

Between What Was and Is Still To Be

Moonlight came for me during the night and took me through my past and future. She held my hand as we traveled star-filled skies and glided above fields of wildflowers.

We rode weightless and free on the backs of winged horses as we viewed days long past when I walked in the sunlit meadows below. My heart was joyful as I relived those days when time stood still, days that were few yet felt like Forever. Darkness suddenly covered the landscape and Forever ended.

I felt heavy with sadness and thought it was over, but then Moonlight brightened again as we passed into a place of purest white light, and I saw endless possibilities ahead filled with magic and music.

I was overwhelmed, so I was slowly taken back to the present. I heard a soft voice whisper that there would be time to experience the magic again, but I had things to finish first. As morning came, Moonlight faded as she said, "I must go now, but I will come back for you when you are ready."

When I woke up, she had left me alone with only her silvery reflection on the water and a song to remind me of the journey through my past and future, suspended between what was and what is still to be.

Sacred Song of the Soul

What should I do when the moonlight wakes me too early with the bright white light that illuminates the landscape and calls for me to come to soak in it? Despite the cool temperatures, I surrender to the invitation as I settle on the deck to greet the day.

Early dawn always offers hope and promise. The new day is not responsible for yesterday's unfinished to-do lists nor its should-haves and disappointments. I anticipate and welcome what each day holds. This morning, I feel a longing in my soul that wants to soar on the soft wind that causes the leaves on the trees to sway as if waltzing.

As dawn breaks and the birds hidden in the forest begin singing their songs, I hear the cardinal begin its cheerful call, quickly answered with clarity and without hesitation from the opposite side. It is as if my feelings have been heard and translated into birdsong.

Like the cardinal's call and mirrored response, there is a sacred calling within the soul that aspires to something higher than the ordinary and longs to be acknowledged. However, unlike the cardinal's consistent early morning song, the soul's call may disappear if not accepted.

That longing is with me today as I reach higher to stay true to my life's purpose. I whisper a prayer that I will always hear that call and surrender to the sacred within.

The River Flows
Where the Forest Ends

Before the Storm

Up before dawn, I sense something is different this morning as I look out the window. There is the river. The trees are still standing. The ridges on the opposite shore are still there and dotted with light from the houses. Then I realize that is the difference. I can see them clearly, even though it's not fully daylight.

The fog has been dense for over a week, covering everything and wrapping itself around the house like a heavy blanket. Some days it was early afternoon before it dissipated. On a few mornings, the sun lit up the fog, and it was like seeing a powerful light shining from behind a heavy canvas.

To see the river, sky, and surrounding landscape this morning was like suddenly having clarity about some life situation that one had been muddling through while trying to reach a solution. But a storm is brewing. I can feel it as I stand with bare feet on the deck. The wind is blowing enough to create sound from the trees. They sway in time with each other, first this way, then that, as if by staying together, they will be safe.

I feel the storm on the wind. The air is heavy and warm, too warm for this time of year. Even though I sense the danger ahead as the storm intensifies, I linger to take in the beauty of morning as it breaks and feel the wonder of being alive to be part of this great mystery.

Advice from a River

As morning light slowly creeps over the ridges, I think of how life subtly changes in the same way. Then one day, we realize this is not the same life we had last year and that change is required. My life has become so vibrant and alive that I wonder whether I am the same person. That is the same river I see daily and the same ridges that create a buffer between me and the world. The same window provides an expansive view that shields me from the cold, and the same chair hugs me warmly.

These things have not changed, but I am different now. I have successfully handled everything life has thrown at me for the past 13 years, which included five years spent rescuing and rehabilitating a person who is so kind and generous that he did not recognize that he was in an abusive situation. The resolution of that situation alone has been liberating, but it does not explain this person who has now emerged and inhabits my body.

In January, I wrote "I think it's time." By September, I knew it was time to make changes. When I spoke those words aloud, that set in motion a series of synchronicities that moved like the current under the river. The surface appears calm and smooth, yet underneath, water from its tributaries mingle to join other rivers that carry them out to sea. Like the river, I can do nothing to stop or redirect where life is taking me.

Yet I still find myself trying to control the flow of my life, but now life pushes my mind out of the way, and my heart seems to be guiding my journey. I do not know where it is taking me, so I will do as the river does and follow life's current and divine timing.

In the Storm

As I opened the door to go outside for my morning quiet time, I could feel the energy of the approaching storm hanging in the air, heavy and waiting. The usual bird calls were absent, and those tentatively singing had moved further inland to the forested area on the other side of the house. The muted calls of the ospreys and great blue herons confirmed they were sheltered in place.

The wind began to blow through the trees, shaking them and separating their canopies and I could see more of the sky. To my surprise, a congregation of water birds had gathered overhead, riding the air currents as if they also wanted the experience of being in the storm.

Dark clouds were forming as lightning and thunder got closer. I questioned my sanity, but I do that often when I feel compelled to experience things because of my curiosity.

I forced myself to linger a while longer as the sky darkened, but the wind-driven rain was like an alarm reminding me that it might be time to go back inside and be in the storm from behind the safety of four walls.

Breathing without Effort

Never has the break of dawn been so heart-stopping beautiful as it is this morning. The sky, with its pink-infused red glow from the rising sun and the indigo clouds, is reflected across the water that is so smooth it's like a mirror stretching from shore to shore. Birds sail low over that water. Are they searching for breakfast or preening at their magnificent reflection in the water's mirror-like surface?

The sky changes yet again even as I write these words; the glow of the morning sun has gone, leaving only dark clouds to compete for reflective space on the water's surface that also mirrors the ridges as reverse images.

It is much like one's life; we are here in this moment, alive, breathing without effort, and planning our day. Just as the sun was there and then vanished, our breath can leave us without giving notice.

I vow to stay focused on the present moment and enjoy what is instead of what was or what might be. The sky and the river are as beautiful in monotone darkness as when the sunlight graced the scene.

But I still want the scene to be as it was when I began writing. How easily the mind strays from one breath to the next.

Watching the Leaves Grow

My usual colorful view has been replaced today with contrasts of dark and light. It is as if the Master Sky Painter wants me to see a different feature of my view today. Even my clothing choice has a message. I am wearing all black, except the white lettering on my sweater that says Count Your Blessings, something I try to practice daily.

The buds on the trees are turning into tiny leaves, and I can almost see them grow. Beyond the distant ridges, the sun backlights the clouds, teasing the sky with its rose-colored light. However, the chill in the air feels as if it is raining somewhere. A few birds have begun their morning song, but it seems lacking in enthusiasm.

I watch the sky as its colors change from dark and light to deep blue, soft pink, orange, and gold. I am counting my blessings that I get to start my days as if I've never seen this divine miracle before.

The sun has scaled the ridges as if on cue, lighting the shadows again. The resident red-tailed hawk calls as if to say don't forget about me. Another day in my forest on the river is underway, bringing new blessings and more tiny leaves.

Night Sounds

I am awake and ready to begin my day, although it is only three in the morning. Glancing out the window fills me with joy because the deck is awash in moonlight, a reward for waking early. So, there's nothing to do except answer the call to the soul from that light but to sit in its glow.

At this time of morning, the sounds of the night and the forest are different than those of the daytime. It takes a few minutes to clear my mind of all thoughts so that I can hear. At first, I hear only the low hum of the night bugs. They are softer, more muted now than the last full moon, a sign that summer is winding down.

The moon is on its descent to the western horizon but still bright enough that I can see the leaves on the trees, and even that faint glimpse tells me that fall is near. Their shapes and volume are shrinking as they prepare for the fiery colors that are coming. The moonlight is bright but it does not block my view of the twinkling stars above me. Then a burned-out one streaks across the sky, giving me time to make a wish.

As my senses have adjusted, I hear the yip of a coyote in the distance, followed closely by dogs barking, and then all is quiet again until I hear something walking through the leaves. It sounds like human footsteps, but then I recognize the steps of a deer, one of many that inhabit the forest along the river.

In the distance, I hear a faint sound from an industrial facility several miles away, but the splash of a fish leaping and falling back into the water quickly wipes out that distraction. A great blue heron squawks as if to express annoyance at the disruption to his sleep.

My senses are overwhelmed with night sounds. It has been too long since I sat in the total dark this way. The sixty-degree temperatures at night are comfortable, and it feels like fall is near.

The moonlight draws me deeper into the mysteries of the night. I allow myself to relax into its glow in gratitude for the opportunity to experience the sounds of the night forest.

Longing

A red-tailed hawk sits in the trees in front of the house daily and watches for his breakfast. He sits there at other times throughout the day but is more visible and vocal in the early morning.

This morning, he called in a way that ripped my heart out. It was not one of his usual calls, not one that entices his prey to come in closer, nor the shrill warning to would-be thieves that want him to drop his catch so they don't have to work so hard for their breakfast. Instead, it was a call that seemed to come from a place within that he holds sacred, something that only he can feel. I felt his longing for something that no longer exists or is just out of reach.

I went outside to offer a ray of hope from a kindred spirit, but he had flown when I reached his special tree. Perhaps a mate answered his call, and he is off for a day of adventure with a friend. I send a silent wish that nothing gets in the way of his eternal hope to fill that longing of his soul.

River Clouds

The river is deceiving this morning, appearing to have no movement. Like a mirror, the water reflects the sky; to the right, it is dark and shadowy like the clouds above. Directly in front of me and to the left, the light from the cloudless part of the sky is reflected on the water, lighting the darkened images of the ridges and trees that appear still on the surface. Then from nowhere, ripples form, creating tiny waves that migrate from the shore toward the pool of light. The images remain reflected on the water's surface, but now it is as if someone dipped a hand in and swirled it around, stirring things up to create dimension and depth.

While my attention is on the mystery in the river, the heavy-looking dark clouds have disappeared. Did they see their dark reflection in the water and send the puff of wind that set their watery images in motion? Where did the clouds go? Perhaps they fell in love with their beauty and dove into the water to bathe in that light, where water and sky appear as one. I long to be a cloud so I can join them.

Song of the Leaves

The breeze is so slight that I can only see the leaves move where they are silhouetted against the faint light of the morning sky. But I hear the hum of their movement as if choreographed to an ancient song from within only they hear.

The air is icy cold, so they likely feel the pending change ahead, signaled by the rapid drop in temperature. They will soon honor the tree that hosts them by displaying vibrant colors of red, gold, and copper, only to have them fall to the forest floor one by one over the coming weeks.

The rustling leaves is the only sound I hear, except for the annoying call of the ever-present crows. Other bird calls are eerily missing. Perhaps they hear the subtle warning in the song of the leaves and are preparing for their trip south. The hummingbirds have long abandoned the feeder I check frequently, hoping to see one more of the tiny miracles before I take it down for the season.

Everything about the morning matches what I feel. Even the golden light that wraps the forest in its glow reflects what I sense. The past few months have been moving me toward a destiny I could not see until recently. But it's been there all along, and just like the song the leaves are singing, I know I will soon join the chorus of change coming from my soul.

Time Is a River

I awoke from dreams that sent me spinning directly into the day without preparation, but it was not the substance that bothered me. It was the leftover feelings.

All I remember of the dream is that I was driving somewhere, trying to get my passenger to some place he needed to go. Yet, upon arrival, it was never the right place for him. Ironically, he was wearing a hat similar to one my hard-to-please father wore.

Puzzling over the meaning of my feelings of frustration and confusion, I sat in the chilly air, savoring the last sips of coffee. The cup was still warm in my hands, but the morning air made me shiver, and I wrapped my sweater closer around me.

I realized the dream was about time and how fast it moves when we are out of alignment with our goals. I was sitting joyfully in this spot only a few days ago, cherishing the hint of fall in the air, which brought relief from the long, hot days of a never-ending summer. Now, I'm shivering. The morning air is like the cold winter months stretched out before me. I have no reason to dread winter. East Tennessee cold spells never last long. So, how is this connected to my feelings from the dream?

Time moves us forward as the river moves toward the sea, carrying water of all the streams it holds on its journey. In contrast, I think about all the things I take with me on my life's voyage that no longer serve a purpose.

Maybe this is what the leftover dream feelings are trying to tell me. Time has brought me to this point of understanding, unceremoniously leaving me in a puddle of emotions that require me to determine what I should no longer carry. Even the river knows it must leave debris that should not be in its water on the banks as it journeys on to the sea.

River of Life

A river is fascinating for many reasons. It holds life within and gives life to all it touches, whether people, plants, or birds. The river is always there, yet it's not the same water that was there yesterday. That river has moved on, joining others as they flow toward the ocean.

It is dark and mysterious while simultaneously reflecting light from the sun and moon or mirroring my face when I get close and gaze into its depth. And if you get close to me, you will see the river reflected in my eyes as I do in yours.

Fall like A Leaf

Pre-dawn on the deck is like receiving a gift to begin each day, one designed just for me. It was so dark that my eyes needed time to adjust, but my other senses were on high alert, especially hearing and feeling.

The morning air was still and chilly, with no sounds other than those of the creatures in the forest. Then I heard what sounded like heavy raindrops on the trees. After listening for a while, I realized it was the sound of hundreds of leaves dropping from the trees, bumping into each other as if they were racing to see which could get to the forest floor first.

A weather change is coming, and the leaves are ready. I sense excitement floating with them in the cold darkness.

I shiver as I comprehend that the exhilaration I have attributed to the leaves reflects emanations from within me as I joyfully anticipate the colorful fall days ahead.

Learning to Let Go

The morning sky just before dawn is a source of inspiration every day. Life is a continuous miracle, and beginning each day by breathing in the morning air both energizes and grounds me for whatever lies ahead that day.

Yesterday the sky was as deep and pure as a black sapphire, a perfect backdrop highlighting the millions of twinkling stars and planets floating across it. I stood almost in the middle of the farm where I grew up, breathing in that miracle of grace as I prepared to be a source of strength for someone who faced health crises.

Today, I am taking it all in from my deck overlooking the river. The sky appears gray, the starlight of yesterday only a memory. And I know there's a new moon up there, but its light is only in my imagination. The miracle is in the sound that I first thought was rain, but as I sit quietly and listen, I realize it is the sound of falling leaves. I can't see them in the darkness, but their sound is one that I learned long ago, maybe while growing up on the farm, or perhaps it's an ancient sound I know deep within my soul.

These are the big leaves that are falling. I can tell from the heaviness of their sound as they strike other leaves. Last week, I watched leaves fall like raindrops as fall begins in earnest. Those smaller leaves fell straight down during heavy rain with no wind. Perhaps the larger ones held on to their trees to oversee the flight of the small ones, perhaps sharing their wisdom of letting go. The leaves did not resist as wind and rain separated them from the trees. I think about times when I have treated some life situation as if it were a battle to fight instead of accepting that it is better to allow it and not struggle against change.

I have learned through observation that whether on the farm or in the forest on the river, life is easier if I accept what it is rather than what I want it to be. Grace guides me back to the source of all wisdom when I struggle with letting go.

Journey of a Leaf

In the faint light of dawn, I watched an oak leaf quiver, still itself, and quiver again, before finally letting go of its grip on the branch that had long ago lost its other leaves. In letting go, the leaf floated on the breeze, weightless, with what seemed like joy at this new freedom. I watched it float about as if considering all its options.

I envisioned myself as a leaf, imagining where I would choose to land, given the freedom to do that. Would I light beneath the tree where I would be close to the others who had shared the tree with me? Would I choose a spot closer to the river where other leaves had landed in the water to catch a ride on a wave that would carry them to a mysterious new land? Or would I allow the breeze to decide where it wants me to be?

As I thought of what it might be like to have such an adventure for myself, I envied the leaf. Time will tell the story of my journey, but the leaf's destination is not mine to tell.

Silence of the Forest

My early morning time on the deck has been eerily quiet this week. There are no bird calls coming from the surrounding forest. The hummingbirds are long gone, their feeders cleaned and packed away for the winter. Even the owls and night bugs are silent. It's as if they have all moved. The only sounds I hear are the hum of wheels on the pavement in the distance as the daily work commute begins and the steady roar of an early morning plane high above, carrying its passengers to someplace far away.

My eyes follow the light and sound of the plane, and I become aware of the splendor above me. The fading night sky is filled with brilliance from the stars and makes up for the lack of birdsong. The dark sapphire of the sky is a perfect canvas for the stars and planets scattered across it. I know all too soon the clouds will return, blanketing my view of these heavenly bodies. So, I breathe it all into my soul for those times when the sky is covered with rain clouds.

But just as the birds return in the spring and fill the forest with song, the sky will clear again, and the light will return. Until then, I am enjoying the eerie silence of the forest around me.

Place of Deep Roots

During a time when news reports and social media are mostly anxiety-producing headlines related to the pandemic, many complain about boredom and being confined at home. I am grateful to live in a serene and inspirational environment and that I have deep roots in a belief that brings me peace.

It is a place where I watch the sun climb above the horizon most mornings. Then hours later, the moon rises in almost the same place, where birdsong fills the morning air to celebrate the new day and where the river reminds me of the rhythm and flow of life as its gentle waves caress the shoreline.

In this space of tranquility, I witness the gray winter of the trees as they slowly develop buds that burst their confinement to offer cool green shade in summer and then turn red and gold in the fall, only to drop to the earth where they nourish their trees until the cycle begins again. Thus grounded, I have faith that anchors me like the roots of the oak trees around me.

After the Storm

The quiet of early dawn is deceiving with its clear sky behind the trees that grow between me and the river. Debris from last night's storm is all over the deck, pieces of trees are everywhere, and the chairs are soaked. My bare feet on the rain-drenched wood connect me to a longing to turn back the time.

While storms of the night have quieted, the leaves on the oaks are still heavy with water creating a dripping sound like that of raindrops. I see no immediate damage, and the trees are still upright, so I breathe again.

I have been on a weekend retreat that was soothing and inspirational, so the intensity of thunder, lightning, heavy rain, and fierce wind of the night's fury is in stark contrast to soft voices reciting mystical poetry.

The retreat was a welcome break from the long hours and sleepless nights of launching the next project. The storms remind me not to get too relaxed because the hard work of writing is only beginning. The morning's clear sky and sunshine are refreshing, and I offer gratitude for the grace of surviving another storm.

Verses and Poems

Embrace the Mystery

As I stand between what was and what is yet to be

I allow the music of life to open my heart

and mind to embrace the possibilities.

Fragments of Morning

The golden glow of sunrise reflected on the water

Red-tailed Hawk calling an early morning greeting

Hummingbird hovering in my face, coming closer
when I reach out

The honk of a lone goose as it flies upriver

Deck squirrel high in the trees, dropping pieces
of breakfast that bounce off the leaves

Fragments of morning beckoning me to breathe
into the grace of another day

I Forgot

In the chilly, rose-gold of sunrise,
I forgot everything else for a moment.

    I forgot to feel burdened by responsibility.

    I forgot about the irrationality of world events,
        the two years of lost time.

    I forgot those who went away, those who broke my heart.

    I forgot yesterday's sadness, yesterday's joy.

For a brief moment, I forgot all of it as I surrendered
    to the divine grace of morning's golden light.

In the Gap

There is a gap between the in-breath and the out-breath.

It is in that space between where

we decide how to navigate the next step.

Remember to breathe.

Jewels in My Heart

The best moments are often unexpected treasures

    sunlight streaming through a dark forest

    watching the first steps of a new-born fawn

    a tiny blue flower peeking through a patch of green

    a pink shell on a quiet beach

    the light in a friend's eyes when she spots you in a crowd

These are jewels of the senses that I wear in my heart.

Late Evening

Light from a sinking sun turns the blue sky orange

Contrails mingle with pale white clouds,

streaking the sky in abstract

The soft breeze that stirs the bare branches of the trees

The crunch of my shoes on the dry grass

A haunting whistle from a distant train

Thoughts of someone far away but always in my heart

Night approaching on silent feet

Peaceful sleep waits to silence my mind

Daylight will return soon

Life will be the same only different

Miracle of Grace

To observe the sunrise one more time

To see a lone star twinkle above the bare treetops where their
    tips lay like eyelashes against the sky

To watch light and dark patterns form on the river
    as the sun rises

To feel the chill in the morning air

To stand barefoot in the pile of leaves nestled against
    the house as if seeking a place to hide from the wind

To hear the soft song of the wind chimes as they bless
    the wind for its caress that sets them free

To smell the aroma floating up from my coffee cup
    and taste its warmth

Mysteries of grace for another day to witness
    these divine miracles of life

Perfect Day

The sun is low in the sky. It will be a perfect day.

I followed the song of the tiny bird that called at sunrise. But the sky suddenly became overcast, and rain began falling as I left for a hike. The rain stopped, and the sun is out again. The day was perfect.

Wildflowers grew in the fields, and butterflies danced on the grasses in the meadows. Sometimes they hitched a ride on my shoulders. The rain began again fifteen minutes from the car; it felt cool on my skin after the climbs in the sun. The day was still perfect.

The sun is sinking low as the day ends. The day has been perfect.

Silence

Sometimes when silence is all
I hear
Pain creeping in.

On silent feet it
Walks about following
Me haunting me
With memories
Until I acknowledge its presence.

It whispers that I should have stayed
In my glass jar
Let you see me but
Hold you at a distance.

The memories are overpowering,
Begging to be heard,
But I
Outwit them.

They slip quietly
Through the window
Defeated, leaving not
A trace they were ever there.

Then all
Is
Silence.

Song of Morning

The tiny bird outside my window sings
the same joyful song, rain or shine.

Dawn breaks and the faint beginning
of sunlight takes away the night's darkness.

The lyrics of the wren's song speak of adventure.

I must go outside and lose myself
in the wonder surrounding me.

The End is the Beginning

Sometimes endings that change into beginnings enter our life so subtly they are not recognizable. Then they stroll so softly that you are on the other side of the passage before you realize you can't go back.

Winter Walking

Icy boards creak beneath my sock-covered feet

Tiny snowflakes of frost sparkle on the glass tabletop

Piercing cold punctuates the morning air

Wind chimes bump stiffly together in numbed song

Leafless trees stand stiffly like concrete poles with limbs

The faint chirping of tiny birds huddled close for warmth

Seagulls sail silently far above without concern

Gray clouds hover in place in the frigid early dawn

Frozen winter landscape beckons me to walk

I will need shoes

Visiting Old Friends

Hiding from Darkness

The fog lifts reluctantly from its
Hiding place in the river, becoming
A gray mist that covers the shoreline and its
Defining boundary of safety.

It creeps silently upward into the tall
Leafless trees of November, and
Wraps them with its gray blanket as if
To warm them from the night's chill.

Then night comes and covers all, the river, the fog,
And the trees, while I wait in vain for the
Light of the full moon that is itself
Hiding behind the night's darkness.

October Lover

October, at once innocent and seductive,
Fiery and cold,
You arrive, riding the heat
Waves of a never-ending summer.

Then you exit on the wind, under the pale light
Of the waning moon, scattering leaves
From fall's painted trees across
The landscape and my soul.

Like a lover finding the weak spot in the heart
Of his Beloved, you light a fire
Then drift away, leaving the white-hot ashes
To tend its warmth until you return.

October, innocent, seductive October,
Farewell, until you come calling again
When you will once more rekindle the
Embers, awakening the fire within me.

Sacred Messages in the Wind

Yesterday life felt heavy, so I whispered
my sorrows into the forest, where Red-tailed Hawk
perched among the red and gold leaves of fall.
He heard my plea and cried
out as if he felt my pain.

Then he took flight grabbing my words
from the air to share them with Eagle
who fishes from the trees along the river.
Eagle, the high-flying messenger
of wisdom and truth, rode the
wind speaking my anguish
to the universe as he soared over land and water.

Today a soft wind rustled the leaves, its breeze like
a caress to get my attention. Red-tailed Hawk had
returned, his call heralding Eagle's
message from the universe. Close your eyes and look
through mine as I fly above it all. You will
see your pain is but an opening to all that connects
to the sacredness of all things.

So I dropped my woes one by one
as trees do their red and gold leaves onto
the forest floor where they will
transform to dirt, nourishing the trees that
shelter these magical purveyors of sacred wisdom.

The Path to My Roots

The leaves are mostly gone now from the old trees along the river. They have shed their leaves so subtly that it's almost unnoticeable. A lone oak leaf floats across my view, and I feel adrift like that leaf as I let go of one way of life to embrace another. I have a sense of time passing and feel an urgency to act quickly.

What has caused this unfamiliar concern with time passing? Life outside my window does not seem concerned about time. The river moves slowly to join others in the ocean. The leaves fall in slow motion from the trees. Quiet slowly settles over the landscape and floats downward to cover the riverbanks. These things feel like peace to me.

Reflecting on the change of seasons made me compare it to those I've experienced in my life. Thoughts of my younger life collided with my current one, reminding me of choices made long ago. There were many paths from which to choose, each one equally appealing. My choices took me away from the places and people that were comforting. But I thrived, made new friends, learned new things, and lived in new places.

Now that I am older, I am pulled back to those places and people I knew before. I had followed where my path led, although it was never clearly marked. I close my eyes and visualize a path that winds and twists through life's terrain, much like my switch-back trail that leads to the river. There were paths within paths, decision points, and rest stops, yet they seemed to be always winding their way back to this river and these old trees.

Like the oak defiantly hanging on to its leaves when all the other trees have let theirs go, the older me hangs on to the certainty that it's not the falling leaves that my life resembles at all; rather, it is their roots. And like those trees, I must trust my roots to hold me to this sacred ground to which I have returned, as I embrace yet another turn on my life's path.

The Space Between

As I have done many times before, I watch night slowly trade places with day, giving up its dark mysteries as dawn slowly illuminates the distant ridges. River and ridges have appeared to be one in their togetherness of darkness and mystery. But as daylight comes, it defines their differences, even as I am still caught up in the mesmerizing exchange of dark and light.

How many times can day and night trade places in this way? How many times can the river pass by me on its way to somewhere else and still be there just the same? How many times can the sun hide its light and still be there to take away the shadows as soon as dark is gone? How many times can a heart break into a million pieces and still be life-giving? How can you be here with me one moment and gone the next?

I reflect on these mysteries as I gaze at the flickering candle in front of me. Its flicker illuminates the tiny replica of an eagle that sits on its perch above the light, its open wings reflected on the ceiling. The reflection dances about and the tiny wings appear to move. The motion makes me wonder—is it poised to take off or land? Is it tomorrow yet, or am I caught forever in this in-between of night and day, dark and light, then and now?

Outside, dawn continues its struggle with night to take control of the sky. The river still moves and the ridges are still dark, yet there is the beginning of blue defining where land stops and sky begins. My heart still beats, though breaking. As night and day once again trade places and sleep becomes waking, I know for now all is well as this circle of thought moves me along in my oneness and separateness with all life. And like dark and light trading places in the sky, I am caught in that space between questioning and accepting the mysteries of my life.

The Truth of Bare Trees in Moonlight

I wait in the coldness of the night for the full moon to rise, anticipating the splendor of its light dancing across the ripples in the river, flickering like tiny candles on the water. This sight fills my soul with joy when the brilliant radiant roundness of the moon finally appears above the distant ridges. There are so many trees between me and the horizon that the moon appears to be climbing their limbs as it makes its way upward into the dark sky, scrambling like a watchman up a ladder to have a look around. This full moon observance is a ritual for me, but tonight I am enchanted by the way the white moonlight washes over the leafless winter trees, illuminating their bark in a way that makes them appear lit from within.

These old trees have seen many full moons have come and gone while they grew from seedlings to a mature forest. They have weathered many storms and witnessed drastic changes in the landscape as they have stood watch by the river. They've watched river barges going to and fro, creating waves that slap against the roots of those nearest the water and carving holes in the earth beneath them. They've shed their leaves through many seasons while quietly nurturing the beginning of new growth that will burst open in spring to become the cool green shade of summer leaves. And then in the fall, those same leaves will turn fiery shades of red, gold, and copper, only to drop to the forest floor, where they become nourishment for the same trees they just abandoned. It is a powerful demonstration of the cycle of life, and I think about how the trees appear throughout the year.

The lush, green ones of spring and summer lean in toward each other like friends do when engaged in shared conversation, and in the quiet of early dawn I can sometimes hear their soft song on the breeze. During storms, however, the trees abandon their leaning-in posture as they sway with the wind as though dancing to music only they can hear. The colors of fall leaves light a fire within me that reaches into the depths of my soul, extracting joyful feelings that are sometimes beyond my ability to express.

But tonight, it is the naked strength and power of the exposed trunks and limbs that are offering a powerful message of truth. Their naked starkness reveals the profound meaning of truth and vulnerability. While their songs of summer are magical, and their fall colors stir my soul, it is the stripped-bare plainness of winter's trees that show me how to stay true to who I am.

Their bare display of what lies underneath the leaves is an example of standing strong when examining the validity of my truth. This courageousness is the basis of my strength just as the bare winter trees are the birthplace for spring's new growth. In the end, it is Truth that I am left with when I strip away the layers of the self I show to the world and stand exposed and vulnerable like bare trees in the moonlight.

Wild Roses

The rose bush grew near the front
steps of the old farmhouse, sprawled
over the rundown fence separating
our place from the neglected one beside us, its fields
filled with tall grasses, blackberry briars, and wildflowers.

Momma called the bush Seven Sisters, with its
blooms of pink and red, huddled
as if to shield themselves from thorns beneath
their leaves. I called the rambling mass Momma's
Roses. The riot of color made her
smile and her smile lit up her sad face.

On the other side, a different rose grew
among the wildflowers and blackberry brambles. No one
noticed these roses, their simple petals
open to catch sunlight or rain; wild and free, strewn
in the meadows of the abandoned homestead.

I called these untamed flowers My Roses. Ignored
by others, they bloomed only for me, gracing
my ordinary days with joy as I walked
to the rickety mailbox at the end
of the dusty road, anticipating its mysterious
contents to be examined on the trek home.

I never told Momma of my love
for the wild roses. I never confessed that
I thought My Roses prettier than her
tame ones because the Seven Sisters made her
smile and that lit up her sad face. I liked
her smile more than any of the summer roses.

Citations

Thanks to the editors, who previously published my work in the last section:

"Hiding from Darkness" — *The Avocet: A Journal of Nature Poetry*, Fall 2018

"October Lover" — *The Avocet: A Journal of Nature Poetry*, Fall 2018

"Sacred Messages in the Wind" — *The Avocet: A Journal of Nature Poetry*, Fall 2019

"The Path to My Roots" was awarded First Place in the 2016 Tennessee Mountain Writers Contest, Inspirational Category, and subsequently published in the 2017 anthology *In God's Hand* by Grace Writers.

"The Space Between" was awarded Second Place in the 2016 Tennessee Mountain Writers Contest, Inspirational Category and subsequently published on social media.

"The Truth of Bare Trees in Moonlight" — *The Weekly Avocet #316*, December 23, 2018

"Wild Roses" — *The Avocet: A Journal of Nature Poetry*, Summer 2021

Sneak Peek from the forthcoming book,
When You Were Mine:
Moving from Pain to Poetry,
by Barbara J Turner

Anticipation

The soft white light of the moon drops below the ridge, blending with the first rays of the morning sun. For a moment, I am in an empty space between yesterday and tomorrow as I forget what has gone before and reach for the tiny thread of what is yet to be with you.

My Heart Fell At Your Feet

For years, I lived half-alive, protecting my heart against the potential pain of another relationship. Then one day, you quietly appeared before me, smiling as we were introduced yet neither of us offered a handshake.

Every wall crumbled, and every sealed window suddenly shattered. You smiled because you knew. My heart escaped and settled on the floor at your feet. I ran from the building because I couldn't breathe.

I forgot to take my heart with me.

The Light in You

I think of you

> when it rains, that silvery soft, slow kind that caresses
> the window pane like someone tapping to come in

> and when the angle of the sun creates a golden light
> like the one surrounding you when we met

Then on a full moon night

> I think of you when moonlight is reflected
> on the water, beaming a path to my door

> and at daylight when the feathers of the Red-tailed
> Hawk catches the sunlight, turning him into a flame

And when you stand close to me, all I see is your light.
Someday, I will tell you about the light.

Author's Note

The personal reflections that make up *Chasing the Butterfly: The Pursuit of Meaning in Everyday Life* are written around the elements of nature, earth, sky, land, and water as well as the creatures that inhabit these places, revealing my surroundings as well as my Appalachian heritage.

My father and paternal grandfather often teamed as sharecroppers as many had done before them, working the bottomlands of the rivers along the Blue Ridge Mountain Range in the Appalachian Mountains. Just prior to my father joining the Navy, his parents bought a nearby farm. Subsequently, my parents also purchased their first farm, thus ending several generations of sharecropping.

While my love of earth and nature came from my paternal side, my creative gift came from my mother. Her father (my grandfather) was a musician known from Bristol to Nashville as an exceptional young guitarist. She was artistic, played piano and organ, and a writer although her work was never published. We often sang songs she had written in church. Her Appalachian heritage is traceable back to eight generations.

My ancestry in the Appalachian Mountains influences my writing and has instilled an inherent appreciation of the universal truths passed down from ancestors who were grounded in place and wisdom. The Tennessee Appalachians are still home to me, and I often return to the place of my early childhood for inspiration, especially when I want to reconnect to my roots.

For more information about my writing and publications, visit my website at www.barbarajturner.com and follow me on social media. It would be an honor if you leave supportive reviews on Amazon, Barnes and Noble, and similar book vendors if you enjoyed reading this book.

Acknowledgements

As a writer, I am blessed to have a wealth of supporters who encourage my writing. I am especially grateful to Ann Davis, Marilyn Kirtley, Elizabeth Maletta, Jennifer Morbitz, and Shirley Raines for consistent support and for comments featured on the cover.

To Beto Cumming, I offer deepest gratitude for the imaginative cover and book design and for serving as proofreader for this project with its many challenges. Above all, I appreciate his assurance that it could be completed in time for my first book signing commitment.

Acknowledgement goes to Joe Long, a longtime friend and reader, who encouraged me regularly in my writing. Joe left his earthly life just prior to publication of this book, but he especially enjoyed the essay "If Only I Could Fly." When he read it, he commented: "I felt as if I was standing on that same spot. My feet are still cold. Barbara Turner speaks to the depths of our souls and always brings such insight into daily life." "If Only I Could Fly" is included in this book and dedicated in his honor.

Finally, I am forever grateful to Larry Long, whom *Chasing the Butterfly: The Pursuit of Meaning in Everyday Life* is dedicated, for his encouragement that always seemed to arrive when I needed it the most. I would be remiss if I did not include Larry's last comments on my work. "I am a composer, and many times while reading your words, I think they should be put to music. It is very obvious to me that the passion with which you write is not only a reflection of a life that has not always worked out as you hoped but also reflects the depth and sincerity of someone who has had to find a way to deal with life when it brings challenges and suffering." I will miss his inspiration.

I am grateful to all of you who read, bought, gifted, and recommended my last book, *Soul Whispers: Listening to the Wisdom Within.* That kind of support to a first-time author is the best encouragement for any writer.